9.24.04 Alissa— Wishing you a heart filled with love now & forever!

BREATHING

QUOTATIONS ON THE MYSTERY OF LOVE

TOGETHER

♡, Pam

RICHARD KEHL

D1112917

DARLING & COMPANY

ISBN 1-883211-84-0

FIRST PRINTING ALL RIGHTS RESERVED PRINTED IN CHINA

DARLING & COMPANY
A DIVISION OF LAUGHING ELEPHANT BOOKS
3645 INTERLAKE AVENUE NORTH SEATTLE WASHINGTON 98103

WWW.LAUGHINGELEPHANT.COM

Do you want me to tell you something really subversive? Love is everything it's cracked up to be. That's why people are so cynical about it...It really is worth fighting for, being brave for, risking everything for. And the trouble is, if you don't risk anything, you risk even more.

ERICA JONG

I am so convinced that love is a nuisance, that I am delighted my friends and I are exempt.

MADAME DE LA FAYETTE

All rivers race to the heat of the heart, where water whispers a name and a place, spreads itself flat, stops waving goodbye and returns to reflect the green shore.

ROSLYN NELSON

The only regret I will have in dying is if it is not for love.

GABRIEL GARCÍA MARQUEZ

All, everything that I understand, I understand only because of love.

LEO TOLSTOY

Love is the child of illusion, and the parent of disillusion.

MIGUEL DE UNAMUNO

BREATHING TOGETHER

There are worse occupations in this world than feeling a woman's pulse.

LAURENCE STERNE

For one human being to love another; that is perhaps the most difficult of all our tasks, the ultimate, the last test and proof, the work for which all other work is but preparation.

RAINER MARIA RILKE

When someone loves you, the way they say your name is different. You know that your name is safe in their mouth.

BILLY AGE 4

Being kissed on the back of the knee is a moth at the window screen.

ANNE SEXTON

...and I laugh and fall dreaming again of the desire...to move openly together in the pull of gravity, which carries the feathered grass a long way down the upbreathing air.

ADRIENNE RICH

What a recreation it is to be in love! It sets the heart aching so delicately, there's no taking a wink of sleep for the pleasure of the pain.

GEORGE COLMAN THE YOUNGER

BREATHING TOGETHER

In a test flight, Saint-Exupéry was to take each aircraft to an altitude of 10,000 feet and fly at full throttle over a three-mile course, noting any difficulties that arose. On his return from one such flight he reported that the aircraft had leaned so severely to one side that he had nearly lost control of it. He was entirely unable to say which way the plane had listed, however. Asked for his flight pad, on which he was meant to record his observations, he displayed a lovely sketch of a woman.

STACY SCHIFF

The heart has its reasons which reason knows nothing of.

BLAISE PASCAL

There is no remedy for love but to love more.

HENRY DAVID THOREAU

To remember...To forgive...To have loved...To be for a moment happy, to have believed...And then in weariness to lean upon the snowy shoulder of oblivion.

MANUEL GUTIERREZ NAJERA

When my desire grows too fierce I wear my bed clothes inside out...

ONO NO KOMACHI

At the touch of love everyone becomes a poet.

PLATO

BREATHING TOGETHER .

Love is not the exclusive province of adolescence, my dear. It's a heart ailment that strikes all age groups. Like my love for you. My love for you is the only malady I've contracted since the usual childhood diseases and it's incurable.

JAY BRATLER, BERNARD SHOENFELD

...sounds she uttered then without meaning yet not meaningless my heartbeat even now echoing them.

ABHINAVAGUPTA - TENTH CENTURY

Lovers read every word three ways; they read between the lines and in the margins...They even take punctuation into account.

MORTIMER J. ADLER

The love we give away is the only love we keep.

ELBERT HUBBARD

I am he that aches with amorous love: Does the earth gravitate? Does not all matter, aching, attract all matter?

WALT WHITMAN

Anyone who says he can see through women is missing a lot.

GROUCHO MARX

Oh, I know, I know. She is dark. And so's the coal before the spark that makes it burn like roses.

ASKLEPIADOS

I close your ear with kisses and seal your nostrils, and round your neck you'll wear - Nay, let me work - a delicate chain of kisses. Like beads they go around, and not one misses to touch its fellow on either side.

D. H. LAWRENCE

We demand the hidden love of everyone we meet. The hidden love, not the daily love.

LEONARD COHEN

It would be impossible to love anyone or anything one knew completely. Love is directed toward what lies hidden in its object.

PAUL VALERY

To be a lover is not to make love, but to find a new way to live.

PAUL LA COUR

Perhaps that is what love is - the momentary or prolonged refusal to think of another person in terms of power.

PHYLLIS ROSE

Where my heart lies, let my brain lie also.

ROBERT BROWNING

Love is so short, forgetting so long.

PABLO NERUDA

BREATHING TOGETHER

If you are ever in doubt as to whether or not you should kiss a pretty girl, always give her the benefit of the doubt.

THOMAS CARLYLE

Love is a hole in the heart.

BEN HECHT

When I see the first new moon faintly in the dusk, I think of the moth eyebrows of a girl I saw only once.

ANONYMOUS

We'll cut the days in two parts. You'll plan the nights (I heard you were not too bad at it), and I'll obey your plans in a very submissive way, and I'll plan the days, and you'll follow me the same way. What do you think of it?

SIMONE DE BEAUVOIR, LETTER TO NELSON ALGREN

It was so cold I almost got married.

SHELLEY WINTERS

Your absence has gone through me like thread through a needle. Everything I do is stitched with its color.

W. S. MERWIN

I teach my sighs to lengthen into songs.

THEODORE ROETHKE

I laughed, tipping back my chair, my hands on the edge of the crisp white tablecloth, and stared at you as if you had just turned a double somersault above the table. The restaurant, buoyant with laughter, made me feel I was falling, not accelerating but floating, like a feather in sunlight. You touched your silverware and stared at the rose in the middle of the table as if it were a photograph.

HENRY BROMWELL

The hardest task in a girl's life is to prove to a man that his intentions are serious.

HELEN ROWLAND

Isn't it the secret intent of this taciturn earth, when it forces lovers together, that inside their boundless emotion all things may shudder with joy?

RAINER MARIA RILKE

Barbara Walters: You've been married forty-two years. What make yours marriage work? Robert Mitchum: Lack of imagination, I suppose.

Since I saw your boat pass up beyond the sun, I have forgotten how to sing and how to paddle the canoe across the lake. I know how to sit down and how to be sad, and I know how to say nothing, but every other art has slipped away.

SONG OF ANNAM

BREATHING TOGETHER

My love has two lives, in order to love you: that's why I love you when I do not love you, and also why I love you when I do.

PABLO NERUDA

The sky where we live is no place to lose your wings. So love, love, love.

HAFIZ

I saved a snowflake for each single hour you were away.

RAINER BRAMBACH

I tried my best, I've sought every loophole of escape, but I am quite unable to avoid the melancholy fact that her thumbs are – lamentable. I am genuinely upset about it for I like her.

W. N. P. BARBELLION

Marriage is a wonderful invention: then again, so is a bicycle repair kit.

BILLY CONNOLLY

The Koran wisely advises: You will be called upon to account for all the permitted pleasures in life you did not enjoy while on earth.

Illusion is the first of all pleasures.

VOLTAIRE

Bring yourself home to me and I will immerse you in every ounce of tenderness I possess.

SABINE

A kiss can be a comma, a question mark or an exclamation point. That's basic spelling that every woman ought to know.

MISTINGUETT

Many a wave would rise on the past towards you; or else, perhaps, as you went by an open window, a violin would be giving itself to someone. All this was a trust. But were you equal to it? Were you not always distracted by expectation, as though all this were announcing someone to love?

RAINER MARIA RILKE

It is for love that I live all alone. Because the lovers I imagine are safer than the ones I've known.

ANONYMOUS

I keep coming back to you in my head, but you couldn't know that, and I have no carbons.

ADRIENNE RICH

Love, she said, should be said more slowly, and ran from the house. Words could not catch her as such. Honesty is so slow, that is the trouble.

UNKNOWN

BREATHING TOGETHER

We are here to learn to endure the beams of love.

WILLIAM BLAKE

The tender pragmatisms of flesh have poetries no enigma,
human or divine, can diminish or demean - indeed, it can
only cause them, and then walk out.

ANONYMOUS

When our hands are alone, they open, like faces. There is
no shore to their opening.

ANONYMOUS

Now the windows are growing blue. I hear a murmuring in
my blood, or else it is the murmur of the gardens down
there...Are you asleep? No. If I put my cheek against yours,
I feel your eyelashes flutter like the wings of a captive
fly...You are not asleep. You are spying upon my excitement.
You protect me against bad dreams; you are thinking of me
as I am thinking of you, and we both feign, out of a strange
sentimental shyness, a peaceful sleep. All my body yields
itself up to sleep, relaxed, and my neck weighs heavily on
your gentle shoulder; but our thoughts unite in love discreetly across this blue dawn so soon increasing.

COLETTE

Love is the triumph of imagination over intelligence.

H. L. MENCKEN

BREATHING TOGETHER

Each divines the secret self of the other, and refusing to believe in the mere daily self, creates a mirror where the lover or the beloved sees an image to copy in daily life; for love also creates the Mask.

WILLIAM BUTLER YEATS

Love from one being to another can only be that two solitudes come nearer, recognize and protect and comfort each other.

HAN SUYIN

The erotic imagination permeates the body, making it transparent. We do not know exactly what it is, except that it is something more. More than history, more than sex, more than life, more than death.

OCTAVIO PAZ

Inadvertently I passed the border of her teeth and swallowed her agile tongue. It lives inside me now like a Japanese fish. It brushes against my heart and my diaphragm as if against the walls of an aquarium. It stirs silt from the bottom.

CZESLAW MILOSZ

The day breaks not, it is my heart.

JOHN DONNE

If you wish to drown, do not torture yourself with shallow water.

BULGARIAN PROVERB

Rilke would have loved you: you never intrude, you never ask questions of those, crying in the dark, who are most near.

DANNIE ABSE

"What's the matter?" she asked, startled. "Can't you sleep?" "I'm only watching you, dear," he said hopelessly.

DORIS LESSING

Ah, from your skin everything comes back to my mouth, comes back to my heart, comes back to my body, and with you I become again the earth that you are: you are a deep spring in me: in you I know again how I am born.

PABLO NERUDA

Love is too young to know what conscience is; yet who knows not conscience is born of love?

WILLIAM SHAKESPEARE

Love is made by two people, in different kinds of solitude.

LOUIS ARAGON

Oh Marguerite! How strange everything is! I kiss you. When shall I see you? I don't know, but I shall see you. How could I not see you? I am beginning to feel that faith that is given to people who fall off towers; they stay hovering for a moment in the air, in some comfortable and magical region where they feel no pain at all. I kiss you, dear heart...

COLETTE

Her eyes are always open. She does not let me sleep. Her dreams in broad daylight make suns evaporate, make me laugh, weep and laugh, and speak without anything to say.

PAUL ELUARD

It is worthwhile falling in love, if only for the parting.

JULIUSZ SLOWACKI

Genuine love is nothing but the attempt to exchange two solitudes.

JOSÉ ORTEGA Y GASSETT

A sad wind came, from invisible worlds... And she, she asked me about things unknowable. And I answered her with unattainable things.

JUAN RAMÓN JIMÉNEZ

Stay a while longer. The butterflies will die and one of us will say "look it is tomorrow already"... and one of us will say, "yes it is still tomorrow."

UNKNOWN

I was a hermit for eight years. I was so afraid I had to belong to myself alone. Now I know I am public property - so I am yours forever.

BRENDA HEFTY

BREATHING TOGETHER

A suave-looking chap invited a young lady to go home with him and see his stamp collection. The girl smiled, shook her head, and said, "Philately will get you nowhere."

AL ROTONDO, QUOTED BY NORTON MOCKRIDGE

Every woman is a science.

JOHN DONNE

Why haven't I thought of it before? This body, remembering yours, is the keepsake you left.

IZUMI SHIKIBU

Our dreams flowed into each other's arms, like streams.

STEPHEN SPENDER

Love from one being to another can only be that two solitudes come nearer, recognize and protect and comfort each other.

HAN SUYIN

The minute I heard my first love story I started looking for you, not knowing how blind that was. Lovers don't finally meet somewhere. They're in each other all along.

RUMI

The most terrible thing of all is happy love, for then there is fear in everything.

COSIMA WAGNER

When Fontenelle, the great French writer, approaching the age of a hundred, discovered Madame Helvétius en déshabille, he exclaimed, "Would I were seventy!"

And if the shadows weren't shadows? If these shadows that I clasp, kiss - that flutter, lit, in my arms, were slender delicate bodies frightened of flesh?

PEDRO SALINAS

Those women who can see their lovers even in dreams are lucky, but without him sleep won't come, so who can dream a dream?

GATHASAPTASATI

For surely, one must be either undiscerning or frightened to love only one person, when the world is so full of gracious and noble spirits.

EDNA ST. VINCENT MILLAY

We always believe that our first love is the last, and that our last love is the first.

GABRIELE D'ANNUNZIO

Passion is sweeter split strand by strand. Divided and re-divided like mercury then gathered up only at the last moment.

JEANETTE WINTERSON

BREATHING TOGETHER

People who throw kisses are mighty hopelessly lazy.

BOB HOPE

Her eyes were like two teaspoonfuls of the Mediterranean.

MICHAEL ARLEN

Let the lover be disgraceful, crazy, absentminded. Someone sober will worry about things going badly. Let the lovers be.

RUMI

Maybe the instant just before the kiss was best of all. I liked when you knew that the kiss was imminent; kisses made me want to use names of parts of flowers: inflorescence, pappus, calyx, anther, pollinator, corolla.

RICK MOODY

Nobody will ever win the battle of the sexes. There's too much fraternizing with the enemy.

HENRY KISSINGER

Love is when a girl puts on perfume and a boy puts on shaving cologne and they go out and smell each other.

KARL ROBERTS AGE 5

An archaeologist is the best husband any woman can have: the older she gets, the more interested he is in her.

AGATHA CHRISTIE

16

BREATHING TOGETHER

Looking back on his marriages, Sacha Guitry commented: "I have always longed to fall into the arms of beautiful women. All I have done is to fall into their hands."

She was everything you say and more. She was the best of my heart for thirty years. She was the music heard faintly at the edge of sound.

RAYMOND CHANDLER

Where you used to be, there is a hole in the world, which I find myself constantly walking around in the daytime, and falling into at night.

EDNA ST. VINCENT MILLAY

I will listen to what you say. You and I can turn and look at the silent river and wait. We know the current is there, hidden; and there are comings and goings from miles away that hold the stillness exactly before us. What the river says, that is what I say.

WILLIAM STAFFORD

When silence speaks for love, she has much to say.

RICHARD GARNETT

The desire to be loved is the last illusion: Give it up and you will be free.

MARGARET ATWOOD

17

BREATHING TOGETHER

All the things of my life I loved and kept on loving through parting, and not through meeting, through pulling away and not through coming together.

MARINA TSVETAEVA

Do you love me because I'm beautiful, or am I beautiful because you love me?

CINDERELLA

Love is the wild card of existence.

RITA MAE BROWN

I have been accused of thinking about women too much... but what could be more beautiful than thinking about women?

AUGUSTE RODIN

A man reserves his true and deepest love not for the species of woman in whose company he finds himself electrified and enkindled, but for that one in whose company he may feel tenderly drowsy.

GEORGE JEAN NATHAN

Were I to put the postcard in a novel, I should have imagined its message as follows: "Thank you for the kiss. It is true, perhaps, that in the middle of the Auvergne I should not have noticed you, or rather recognized, had you not, just before kissing me, slightly tilted your straw hat to the left. Ann."

KENNETH KOCH

BREATHING TOGETHER

When we emerge from a period of falling in love, we feel an impression similar to awakening from a narrow passage crammed with dreams.

JOSÉ ORTEGA Y GASSET

I can't mate in captivity.

GLORIA STEINEM

While thinking of his Dollie - his pillow catches fire.

ALBERT EINSTEIN

"Leonie, you will do well to consider. You are not the first woman in my life." She smiled through her tears. "Monsigneur, I would so much rather be the last woman, than the first," she said.

GEORGETTE HEYER

One doesn't die from love. Sometimes one dies from another's love when he buys a revolver.

MARCEL PAGNOL

Even dreams cannot cross over the vast mountains that divide us. And this eternal longing can turn a heart to dust.

LI PO

No, never forget!...Never forget any moment: they are too few.

ELIZABETH BOWEN

BREATHING TOGETHER

My love for you tonight is so deep and tender that it seems to be outside myself as well. I am shut up fast like a little lake in the embrace of some big mountains, you would see me down below, deep and shining - and quite fathomless, my dear. You might drop your heart into me and you'd never hear it touch bottom.

KATHERINE MANSFIELD

For the lips that kissed me, these tender, cool, impersonal lips are the same as yesterday and their ineffectiveness annoys me...But suddenly they change and I no longer recognize the kiss: it becomes lively, demanding, then tender, and then again feverish, withdraws a little and again becomes more urgent and rhythmic and suddenly it pauses, as if waiting for an answer that does not come...

COLETTE

We had a lot in common. I loved him and he loved him.

SHELLEY WINTERS

To be loved, certainly, is different from being admired, as one can be admired from afar, but to really love someone it is essential to be in the same room with the person, crouching behind the drapes.

WOODY ALLEN

He can't whisper, he can't tiptoe, and he won't hurry.

MARY GRAY, OF HER HUSBAND, DIXIE

BREATHING TOGETHER

Now that I have your face by heart, I look. Now that I have your voice by heart, I read. Now that I have your heart by heart, I see.

LOUISE BOGAN

Love does not consist in gazing at each other but in looking together in the same direction.

ANTOINE DE SAINT-EXUPÉRY

I would like to be the air that inhabits you for a moment only. I would like to be that unnoticed and that necessary.

MARGARET ATWOOD

Oh, Charles - a woman needs certain things. She needs to be loved, wanted, cherished, sought after, cosseted, pampered. She needs sympathy, affection, devotion, understanding, tenderness, infatuation, adulation, - that isn't much to ask, Charles.

BARRY TOOK AND MARTY FELDMAN

I shall be the shepherd of your hair. A dawn made of all the air I ever breathed.

SAINT GERAUD

A man now, aging, I know the best of love is not to bestow, but to recognize.

HAYDEN CARRUTH

BREATHING TOGETHER

Art is the accomplice of love.

JAN STANTON HITCHCOCK

We embraced each other with - how to say it? - a momentous smiling calm, as if the cup of language had silently over-flowed into these eloquent kisses which replaced words like the rewards of silence itself, perfecting thought and gesture.

LAWRENCE DURRELL

It's this way: being captured is beside the point. The point is not to surrender.

NAZIM HIKMET

The burned lip will always spurn the flame.

HUGH MORRIS

You shall not find a heart without losing the heart.

RUMI

Then I did the simplest thing in the world. I leaned down and kissed him. And the world cracked open.

AGNES DE MILLE

A kiss is a lovely trick designed by nature to stop speech when words become superfluous.

INGRID BERGMAN

Some people claim that marriage interferes with romance. There's no doubt about it. Anytime you have a romance, your wife is bound to interfere.

GROUCHO MARX

Your hands hold roses always in a way that says they are not only yours.

RICHARD WILBUR

Where the mist has torn the hills are the colors of spring. The sky is whitening. Not many stars are left. The fragment of moon is going out but your face in the early light glitters. Now we must separate.

NIU HSI CHI

Love, my dear Gigi, is a thing of beauty like a work of art. And, like a work of art, it is created by artists. The greater the artist, the greater the art.

ALAN JAY LERNER

When she raises her eyelids it's as if she were taking off all her clothes.

COLETTE

When a man watches over a sleeping woman, he tries to understand. When a woman watches over a sleeping man, she thinks about eating him in a delicious sauce.

PABLO PICASSO

BREATHING TOGETHER

Love and Love always read together from the same book, but not always the same page.

RICHARD GARNETT

I love in you a someone that only I have discovered...

GUY DE MAUPASSANT

For me the initial delight is the surprise of remembering something I didn't know I knew.

ROBERT FROST

Taking the hands of someone you love, you see they are delicate cages.

ROBERT BLY

The person one loves never really exists, but is a projection focused through the lens of the mind onto whatever screen it fits with least distortion.

ARTHUR C. CLARKE

Love doesn't just sit there, like a stone, it has to be made, like bread, remade all the time, made new.

URSULA LE GUIN

Perfect love means to love the one through whom one became unhappy.

SØREN KIERKEGAARD

BREATHING TOGETHER

It is only with the heart that one can see rightly; what is essential is invisible to the eye.

ANTOINE DE SAINT-EXUPÉRY

This heart, longing for you, breaks to a thousand pieces – I wouldn't lose one.

IZUMI SHIKIBU

Mariolle's eyes always searched among the letters for the longed-for handwriting...What could she say? Would the word 'love' be there? She had never yet used that word without adding 'well' or 'very much;' 'I love you well' or 'I love you very much.' How thoroughly he was used to this formula that lost all power by using additional words! Can there be much or little in loving?

GUY DE MAUPASSANT

Every biologist can tell you what love is. Only the biologist who is in love does not know.

GYULA FEKETE

The little I want, you never bring it. I miss it; that's why I lay claim to so much. To so many things, to infinity almost...because of that little bit that's missing, that you never bring.

HENRI MICHAUX

BREATHING TOGETHER

He kissed me and now I am somebody else.

GABRIELA MISTRAL

I've always loved the back of your neck, the only part of you I could look at without being seen.

FRANÇOIS TRUFFAUT

I don't want to live - I want to love first, and live incidentally.

ZELDA FITZGERALD

...The act of balance. If the heart is on the left, lean the head slightly to the right, keep your pockets empty, make no big gestures - leave all rhetoric behind...

TOMAS TRANSTRÖMER

In my mouth I keep your thirst.

JUAN RAMÓN JIMÉNEZ

As she slept, her head on my arm, I leaned over to look at her face, which was surrounded by flames. I was playing with fire. I became aware that my lips were on hers. Her eyes were still closed, but she was quite obviously not asleep. I kissed her, amazed at my boldness, whereas in fact it was she who had drawn my head towards her mouth. Her hands clung to my neck: they would not have held me so fast in a shipwreck. And I did not understand whether she wanted me to save her or to drown with her.

RAYMOND RADIGUET

I could easily kill my rival, but that would upset the Duchess too much.

COLONEL ROMANELLI, WHO KILLED HIMSELF IN NAPLES BECAUSE
THE DUCHESS HAD LEFT HIM, QUOTED BY STENDHAL

...a final comfort that is small, but not cold: the heart is the only broken instrument that works.

T. E. KALEM

All my body yields itself to sleep, relaxed, and my neck weighs heavily on your gentle shoulder; but our thoughts unite in love discreetly across this blue dawn, so soon increasing.

COLETTE

Love is a species of melancholy.

ROBERT BURTON

The song with nothing to say has gone to sleep on my lips.

DONALD JUSTICE

...my love now knew only the heart-rending nostalgia for what it lacked: a where, a surrounding, a before, an after.

ITALO CALVINO

My hands have given their gift. Then themselves.

WILLIAM STAFFORD

BREATHING TOGETHER

When with you asleep, I plunge into your mind, and I listen, with my ear on your naked breast, to your tranquil heart, it seems to me that, in its deep throbbing, I surprise the secret of the center of the world.

JUAN RAMÓN JIMÉNEZ

To make a prairie it takes a clover and one bee. One clover and a bee, and reverie. The reverie alone will do, if bees are few.

EMILY DICKINSON

Come she said. Stay she said. Smile she said. Die she said. I came. I stayed. I smiled. I died.

NAZIM HIKMET

If you do not hear from me again, you are not listening.

JACK MARSHALL

To put it simply, one is changed by what one loves, sometimes to the point of losing one's entire identity.

JOSEPH BRODSKY

Love which is all-inclusive seems to repel us.

HENRY MILLER

I don't know. When my lover comes to me and says such loving things, do all my parts become eyes or ears?

AMARUSATAKA

Because of this, Love, tie me to a purer motion, to the constancy that beats in your chest with the wings of a swan underwater, so that our sleep might answer all the sky's starry questions with a single key.

PABLO NERUDA

Money cannot buy love, but it makes shopping for it a lot easier.

ANONYMOUS

We only keep what we lose.

MAY SARTON

He is a chump, you know. That's what I love about him. That and the way his ears wiggle when he gets excited.

P. G. WODEHOUSE

We need, in love, to practice only this: letting each other go. For holding on comes easily; we do not need to learn it.

RAINER MARIA RILKE

Love is like an hourglass, with the heart filling up as the brain empties.

JULES RENARD

I want to do with you what spring does with the cherry trees.

PABLO NERUDA

BREATHING TOGETHER

It takes patience to appreciate domestic bliss; volatile spirits prefer unhappiness.

GEORGE SANTAYANA

I kissed my first woman and smoked my first cigarette on the same day. I have never had time for tobacco since.

ARTURO TOSCANINI

As soon as you cannot keep anything from a woman, you love her.

PAUL GERALDY

My definition of love is: the need to be with.

NED ROREM

The moon asked me to meet her in a field tonight. I think she has amorous ideas.

HAFIZ

The poet is one who, because he cannot love, imagines what it would be like if he could.

JAMES DICKEY

There lives within the very flame of love a kind of wick or snuff that will abate it.

WILLIAM SHAKESPEARE

BREATHING TOGETHER

Sensual pleasure passes and vanishes in the twinkling of an eye, but the friendship between us, the mutual confidence, the delight of the heart, the enchantment of the soul, these things do not perish and can never be destroyed. I shall love you until I die.

VOLTAIRE TO MME. DENIS

I know how he dreams me. I know because I dream his dreams.

ROSELLEN BROWN

Yes. Yes. My life was going to be, and already was, a shore set adrift. But when you woke up, you drowned me in your eyes.

RAFAEL ALBERTI

The eyes are the silent tongues of love.

MIGUEL DE CERVANTES

Vivacious 42-year-old divorcee seeks male companion with similar personality for evenings out, must have own teeth.

AN ADVERTISEMENT FROM THE LAKELAND ECHO, 1985

We can only learn to love by loving.

IRIS MURDOCH

Why is it better to love than be loved? It is surer.

SACHA GUITRY

BREATHING TOGETHER

What constitutes adultery is not the hour which a woman gives her lover, but the night which she afterwards spends with her husband.

GEORGE SAND

One makes mistakes, that is life. But it is never quite a mistake to have loved.

ROMAIN ROLLAND

Love's a fire, but whether it's going to warm your heart or burn down your house, you never can tell.

JOAN CRAWFORD

When he comes back to my arms I'll make him feel what nobody ever felt...me vanishing into him like water into the clay of a new jar.

HEMACANDRA

When Albert Einstein, on a visit to the California Institute of Technology in the nineteen-thirties, was told by the great American geneticist Thomas Morgan of his hope of bringing physics and chemistry to bear on what were then some of the major biological puzzles, Einstein is said to have replied, "No, this trick won't work...How on earth are you ever going to explain in terms of chemistry and physics so important a biological phenomenon as first love?"

JEREMY BERNSTEIN

BREATHING TOGETHER

I've never been able to work without a woman to love. Perhaps I'm cruel. They are earth and sky and warmth and light to me. I'm like an Irish peasant, taking potatoes out of the ground. I live by the woman loved. I take from her. I know damned well I don't give enough.

SHERWOOD ANDERSON

To love and win is the best thing; to love and lose, the next best.

WILLIAM MAKEPEACE THACKERAY

If love takes even a sixty-year-old by surprise, imagine what it can do to a twenty-year-old.

MARIA GUSTAAVA JOTUNI

If you take my heart by surprise, the rest of my body has the right to follow.

JOHN OSBORNE

"How have you come to be so thin? Why are you trembling? Why are you so pale, oh simple girl?" And she answered the lord of her life "all these things just happen for no reason," sighing as she said it and turning to let tears fall.

500 B.C. - 1000 A.D. CLASSICAL SANSKRIT

A shudder of love for him, and no way to show it. She worries and worries, and finds her heart unchanged: over and over when she sleeps the butterfly's imprisoned in her dreams.

OU-YANG HSIU

Now, as ever, you fill me with love and sorrow; if any tear is left me, I quicken it to wash our two obscurities.

RAMON LOPEZ VELARDE

I know nothing of anything in the future, but I love for the sake of loving, and I shall die of love.

PAUL ELUARD

A happy marriage is a long conversation which always seems too short.

ANDRÉ MAUROIS

An elementary particle is not an independently existing unanalyzable entity. It is, in essence, a set of relationships that reach outward to other things.

H.P. STAPP

She felt a little stir of something that came over her like a flush, a sort of inner buoyancy, and she lifted her face to kiss the warm blade of his cheekbone.

ANNE TYLER

There will always be a battle between the sexes because men and women want different things. Men want women and women want men.

GEORGE BURNS

Basically my wife was immature. I'd be at home in the bath and she'd come in and sink my boats.

WOODY ALLEN

When you love somebody, your eyelashes go up and down and little stars come out of you.

KAREN AGE 7

It takes a lot of experience for a girl to kiss like a beginner.

ANONYMOUS

… and he caught her in his arms, held her fast there, felt her lashes beat his cheek like netted butterflies.

EDITH WHARTON

Our love is like the misty rain that falls softly but floods the river.

AFRICAN PROVERB

We are first aware of love when we realize we are dependent on someone else for our happiness.

JILLY COOPER

This was not a young man making love to a girl. This was the meeting of twin souls. The light covering of flesh was so transmuted with ecstasy that earthly passion became a heavenly embrace of white, fiery flame.

ISADORA DUNCAN

BREATHING TOGETHER

It is the special quality of love not to be able to remain stationary, to be obliged to increase under pain of diminishing.

ANDRÉ GIDE

Love is purely a creation of the human imagination ... the most important example of how the imagination continually outruns the creature it inhabits.

KATHERINE ANNE PORTER

Not to believe in love is a great sign of dullness. There are some people so indirect and lumbering that they think all real affection must rest on circumstantial evidence.

GEORGE SANTAYANA

... that pane of glass called passion ... It may distort things at times, but it's wonderfully convenient.

FRANÇOISE SAGAN

I can see from your utter misery, from your eagerness to misunderstand each other, and from your thoroughly bad temper, that this is the real thing.

PETER USTINOV

It is as absurd to say that a man cannot love one woman all the time as it is to say that a violinist needs several violins to play the same piece of music.

HONORÉ DE BALZAC

It doesn't much signify whom one marries, for one is sure to find out the next morning that it was someone else.

SAMUEL ROGERS

The head never rules the heart, but just becomes its partner in crime.

MIGNON MCLAUGHLIN

Do you know why we divorced? ... We would go to the movies your father and I ... and I'd come out being Carole Lombard only he refused to be Humphrey Bogart.

SUSAN GRIFFIN

A kiss that speaks volumes is seldom a first edition.

ANONYMOUS

It's impossible to kiss a girl unexpectedly—only sooner than she thought you would.

ANONYMOUS

Your absence has not taught me how to be alone, it merely has shown that when together we cast a single shadow on this wall.

DOUG FETHERLING

You know what charm is: a way of getting the answer without having asked a clear question.

ALBERT CAMUS

She wanted to be the reason for everything and so was the cause of nothing.

DJUNA BARNES

Love is a mystery which, when solved, evaporates.

NED ROREM

I hold this to be the highest task of a bond between two people: that each should stand guard over the solitude of the other.

RAINER MARIA RILKE

I came upon no wine so wonderful as thirst.

EDNA ST. VINCENT MILLAY

There is no more disturbing experience in the rich gamut of life than when a man discovers, in the midst of an embrace, that he is taking the episode quite calmly… He doesn't know, now, whether it's love or passion. In fact, in the confusion of the moment, he's not quite sure if it isn't something else altogether, like forgery.

E.B. WHITE

Tomorrow we shall give them only a leaf from the tree of our love, a leaf that will fall upon the earth as if our lips had made it, like a kiss that falls from our invincible heights to show the fire and the tenderness of a true love.

PABLO NERUDA

The real genius for love lies not in getting into, but in getting out of love.

GEORGE MOORE

Sudden love is latest cured.

JEAN DE LA BRUYÈRE

It hurts me to say it, but I'd have given ten conversations with Einstein for a first meeting with a pretty chorus girl.

ALBERT CAMUS

There you are you see, quite simple. If you cannot have your dear husband for a comfort and a delight, for a bread-winner and a crosspatch, for a sofa, chair, or hot-water bottle, one can use him as a Cross to be borne.

STEVIE SMITH

The lover, who has not felt the hot tears rise at the sight of some slight, infinitely poignant imperfection in the body of the beloved, has never loved.

M. LEVY

It is our own mediocrity that makes us let go of love, makes us renounce it. True love doesn't know the meaning of renunciation.

EUGÈNE IONESCO

BREATHING TOGETHER

You need somebody to love while you're looking for someone to love.

SHELAGH DELANEY

Some people ask the secret of our long marriage. We take time to go to a restaurant two times a week. A little candlelight, dinner, music and dancing. She goes on Tuesdays. I go Fridays.

HENNY YOUNGMAN

Love is made of two people, in different kinds of solitude.

LOUIS ARAGON

Many promising reconciliations have broken down because, while both parties came prepared to forgive, neither party came prepared to be forgiven.

CHARLES WILLIAMS

The beginning, middle, and end of love is – a sigh.

ARNOLD HAULTAIN

And never, ever, no matter what else you do in your whole life, never sleep with anyone whose troubles are worse than your own.

NELSON ALGREN

BREATHING TOGETHER

Let there be spaces in your togetherness.

KAHLIL GIBRAN

If you haven't had at least a slight poetic crack in the heart, you have been cheated by nature.

PHYLLIS BATTELLE

To keep the fire burning brightly there's one easy rule: Keep the two logs together, near enough to keep each other warm and far enough apart - about a finger's breadth - for breathing room.

MARNIE REED CROWELL

Most marriages recognize this paradox: Passion destroys passion; we want what puts an end to wanting what we want.

JOHN FOWLES

A man nearly always loves for other reasons than he thinks. A lover is apt to be as full of secrets from himself as is the object of his love from him.

BEN HECHT

Love is whatever you can still betray ... Betrayal can only happen if you love.

JOHN LE CARRÉ

BREATHING TOGETHER

The love that lasts longest is the love that is never returned.

W. SOMERSET MAUGHAM

A successful marriage requires falling in love many times, always with the same person.

MIGNON MCLAUGHLIN

The first duty of love is to listen.

PAUL TILLICH

I have learned the guilt of indifference. The opposite of love is not hate but indifference.

ELIE WIESEL

You're beautiful, like a May fly.

ERNEST HEMINGWAY

To say the truth, reason and love keep little company together now-a-days.

WILLIAM SHAKESPEARE

We are adhering to life now with our last muscle – the heart.

DJUNA BARNES

The heart is forever inexperienced.

HENRY DAVID THOREAU

BREATHING TOGETHER

The fickleness of the women I love is only equaled by the infernal constancy of the women who love me.

GEORGE BERNARD SHAW

We turned on one another deep, drowned gazes, and exchanged a kiss that reduced my bones to rubber and my brain to gruel.

PETER DE VRIES

They (the Shoshone) know that it (romantic love) exists. But they also recognize it for what it is – in their case, a form of madness.

PETER FARB

On the whole, love comes with the speed of light; separation, with that of sound.

JOSEPH BRODSKY

Love transforms; it simultaneously makes us larger and limits our possibilities.

MICHAEL DORRIS

Love. The black hook. The spear singing through the mind.

LOUISE ERDRICH

Love is more afraid of change than destruction.

FRIEDRICH NIETZSCHE

BREATHING TOGETHER

We are not the same persons this year as last; nor are those we love. It is a happy chance if we, changing, continue to love a changed person.

W. SOMERSET MAUGHAM

Those whose suffering is due to love are, as we say of certain invalids, their own physicians.

MARCEL PROUST

It is the missed opportunity that counts, and in a love that vainly yearns from behind prison bars, you have perchance the love supreme.

ANTOINE DE SAINT-EXUPÉRY

We must try to love one another… The terrible and beautiful sentence, the last, the final wisdom… is remembered at the end, is spoken too late, wearily. It stands there, awful and untraduced, above the dusty racket of our lives. Not forgetting, no forgiving, no denying, no explaining, no hating.

THOMAS WOLFE

Lovers who love truly do not write down their happiness.

ANATOLE FRANCE

I suppose I shall marry eventually. One does that, one drifts into stability.

PETER DE VRIES

BREATHING TOGETHER

Women like silent men. They think they're listening.

MARCEL ACHARD

The women I have loved I have desired for themselves, but also because I feared myself.

CARLOS FUENTES

The return makes one love the farewell.

ALFRED DE MUSSET

We distrust our heart too much, and our head not enough.

JOSEPH ROUX

Let us not burden our remembrance with a heaviness that's gone.

WILLIAM SHAKESPEARE

I don't know whether it's normal or not, but sex has always been something that I take seriously. I would put it higher than tennis on my list of constructive things to do.

ART BUCHWALD

Most creatures have a vague belief that a very precarious hazard, a kind of transparent membrane, divides death from love; and that profound idea of nature demands that the giver of life should die at the moment of giving.

MAURICE MAETERLINCK

BREATHING TOGETHER

Retrospectively, I would agree with Luis Buñuel that sex without sin is like an egg without salt.

CARLOS FUENTES

I have a simple principle for the conduct of life – never to resist an adequate temptation.

MAX LERNER

An orange on the table. Your dress on the rug. And you in my bed. Sweet present of the present, cool of night, warmth of my life.

JACQUES PRÉVERT

It is a mistake to speak of a bad choice in love, since, as soon as a choice exists, it can only be bad.

MARCEL PROUST

All day today I die. I die eternally losing myself in joy. By one touch you put out time.

CAROLYN KIZER

Go, sighs, go there where you go always, and if she is sleeping, my little one, forget her.

LOPE DE VEGA

I've sometimes thought of marrying, and then I've thought again.

NOEL COWARD

When the girl's family showed him the door with the words "Your persistence is disgusting," Vincent Van Gogh turned to the lamp on the table, put his hand into the flame, and said, "Let me see her, then, for just as long as I can hold my hand in this flame."

ARISTOTLE DELANCEY

Without you I can't live with the part of me that wants to live without you.

RUTH BURNS

Love is an attempt to change a piece of a dream world into reality.

THEODOR REIK

There is love of course. And then there's life, its enemy.

JEAN ANOUILH

There is very little difference between men and women in space.

HELEN SHARMAN – BRITAIN'S FIRST ASTRONAUT IN SPACE.

A life without love, without the presence of the beloved, is nothing but a mere magic-lantern show. We draw out slide after slide, swiftly tiring of each, and pushing it back to make haste for the next.

GOETHE

BREATHING TOGETHER

There is only one way to be happy by means of the heart –
to have none.

PAUL BOURGET

Sex is one of the nine reasons for reincarnation. The other
eight are unimportant.

HENRY MILLER

There is nothing safe about sex. There never will be.

NORMAN MAILER

That is what I imagine love to be: Incompleteness in absence.

EDMOND AND JULES DE GONCOURT

Once the realization is accepted that even between the
closest human beings infinite distances continue to exist, a
wonderful living side by side can grow up, if they succeed
in loving the distance between them which makes it possible
to see the other whole against the sky.

RAINER MARIA RILKE

For years I shall remember how you came down to Seaford
House in your electric brougham. That vehicle is forever
enshrined in my memory. You can never ... form any idea
of the wonder it is to me to see you – to think you and to
dream you.

GEORGE MOORE – LETTER TO LADY CUNARD

I look down the tracks and see you coming – and out of the haze and mist your darling rumpled trousers are hurrying to me.

ZELDA FITZGERALD – LETTER TO F. SCOTT FITZGERALD

Love lives on words and dies with deeds.

MARINA TSVETAYEVA

My old teacher (Roshi) has said; "The older you get, the lonelier you become, and the deeper love you need."

LEONARD COHEN

Connecting may well be what the universe does best – even exclusively.

K.C. COLE

Why is a light ray so fast and a whisper so slow?

UNKNOWN

Love: The skillful audacity required to share an inner life.

GERTRUDE STEIN

My wife and I tried two to three times in the last forty years to have breakfast together, but it was so disagreeable that we had to stop.

WINSTON CHURCHILL

BREATHING TOGETHER

Passion will obscure our sense so that we eat sad stuff and call it nectar.

WILLIAM CARLOS WILLIAMS

Unexpectedly, one winter evening, Benjamin Franklin met a woman to whom he had made love some months before. A trifle hurt, she said, "You haven't seen me all summer. I fear you no longer desire me." "Madam, nothing could be farther from the truth," Franklin replied. "I've merely been waiting for the nights to get longer."

There is always something left to love. And if you ain't learned that, you ain't learned nothing.

LORRAINE HANSBERRY

Love is like a reservoir of kindness and pleasure, like silos and pools during a siege.

YEHUDA AMICHAI

A love song that cannot bear its own music hovers over the love's silence.

HAN YONG-WOON

I think, "At least in my dreams we'll be able to meet ..." Moving my pillow this way and that on the bed, completely unable to sleep.

IZUMI SHIKIBU

BREATHING TOGETHER

Words, phrases, syllables, stars that turn around a fixed center. Two bodies, many beings that meet in a word. The paper is covered with indelible letters that no one spoke, that no one dictated, that have fallen there and ignite and burn and go out. This is how poetry exists, how love exists.

OCTAVIO PAZ

Love is a springtime plant that perfumes everything with it's hope, even the ruins to which it clings.

GUSTAVE FLAUBERT